Cheltenham In Camera

by Guy Kilminster

QUOTES LIMITED of BUCKINGHAM

MCMXCI

Published by Quotes Limited
Buckingham, England

Typeset in Plantin by
Key Composition, Northampton, England

Pictures Lithographed by
South Midlands Lithoplates Limited, Luton, England

Printed by Busiprint Limited
Buckingham, England

Bound by Charles Letts Limited
Edinburgh, Scotland

ISBN 0 86023 387 1

Acknowledgements

A number of people have helped me with the writing of this book. I should like to thank Dr Steven Blake, the Deputy Director and Keeper of Social History at Cheltenham Art Gallery and Museum, for his advice and support. Many thanks are also due to the staff of Cheltenham Reference Library who have allowed me access to the Local Studies Collection.

My brother Greg has been of great assistance, reading, editing and commenting upon the text and my wife Julie has helped with proof-reading and typing.

Finally I wish to thank all those people who have donated photographs to Cheltenham Museum over the last 90 years. Without their forethought these views of the town's past would have been lost.

All photographs are reproduced with the kind permission of Cheltenham Art Gallery and Museum.

The following books have been consulted during the preparation of *Cheltenham In Camera*:

Blake, S. T. *Cheltenham's Churches and Chapels* (Cheltenham Art Gallery and Museum 1979)

Blake, S. T. and Beacham, R. *The Book of Cheltenham* (Barracuda Books, Buckingham 1982)

Burrow, E. *Cheltenham: The Midland Educational and Health Centre* (1897)

Cavell, John *The Story of Christ Church* (1962)

Cheltenham Annuaires and Directories 1850-1920

Cheltenham Guide Books

Clarke, A. K. *A History of Cheltenham Ladies' College* (John Catt Ltd 3rd Edition 1979)

Fletcher, Simona 'Cheltenham's first photographers 1841-1858' Cheltenham Local History Society *Journal* 3 (1985)

Hallett, Michael *Professional Photographers in Cheltenham 1841-1914* (Royal Photographic Society Historical Supplement, draft manuscript 1986)

Hart, Gwen *A History of Cheltenham* (1965)

Miller, Eric *The History of Leckhampton Church* (1989)

Morgan, M. C. *Cheltenham College: the first hundred years* (1968)

Pakenham, Simona *Cheltenham: a biography* (Macmillan 1971)

Woodward, J. *Cheltenham Rugby Football Club* (1989)

Wyndham-Quin, W. H. *The Yeomanry Cavalry of Gloucester and Monmouth* (1898)

Today it is likely that almost every household in the country has a camera. Pictures are taken of family and friends, holidays, weddings and other special occasions. They remind us of places visited and people we have known. It is difficult for us, so familiar with both camera and photograph, to understand the wonder and excitement that the invention of photography generated over 150 years ago.

In 1839, when the first announcements were made about the discovery of the photographic process, Cheltenham was at its height as a spa resort. There were six spas in the town, to which people flocked to take the waters. Although the medicinal qualities of the waters were widely praised, the visitors also enjoyed a round of social engagements and entertainments, guaranteed to encourage even the perfectly healthy to return to the town.

Until the late 18th century, Cheltenham had been a small town, a market centre for the surrounding countryside. The mineral waters were first discovered in 1716 and commercial exploitation began in the 1730s. Unfortunately this was not a great success and there was little effect on the prosperity or growth of the town.

The event that was to forever change Cheltenham occurred in 1788. George III and his family spent five weeks in the town, to allow the King to take the waters. Although they failed to have a beneficial effect on him, the impact of the Royal visit was tremendous. Cheltenham was suddenly fashionable, the place to visit.

The subsequent demand for the waters led to new wells being opened. As the number of visitors increased, there was also a need for more accommodation. Consequently, residential estates were built and hotels opened.

By 1840 Cheltenham was both an established spa resort and a popular place of retirement. It was in this prosperous town that a Mr John Palmer opened his Photographic Institution in September 1841. Palmer had bought a licence off Richard Beard, an artist who had opened the first European photographic portrait studio in London, six months earlier. Beard was overwhelmed by the demand for portraits. This encouraged him to buy the patent rights to the process that produced photographic images known as daguerrotypes. He was then able to control the setting up of studios in other towns.

According to contemporary newspaper reports, Palmer's studio was also an overnight success. To people familiar with portraits painted by artists, the production of a true likeness of a person, through a wooden box and a lens, was nothing short of miraculous. With each framed or cased picture costing a guinea (£1.05) however, it was only the wealthy who could afford to be photographed. In Cheltenham the well-to-do residents no doubt vied with each other, to be the first to have their pictures taken.

As technical developments occurred, the photographic process steadily improved. In about 1860, the 'carte-de-visite' became popular. Twelve prints could be produced from one studio sitting, dramatically reducing the cost of having a photograph taken. 'Cartomania' developed among the Victorian middle classes. People compiled albums of 'cartes', placing pictures of family and friends beside those of politicians, stars of the stage, Queen Victoria and her family, which were now commercially produced. As the demand for portrait photography increased, so did the number of photographic studios.

It was also during the 1860s that the travel view or topographical photograph became popular. Photographers travelled abroad to places such as Egypt, the Holy Land, India and China. The pictures that they took provided a curious public with their first sight of these distant countries, and the photographs were avidly collected.

Towns and landscapes in Britian were the next subjects to which the commercial photographers turned their cameras. With more people travelling further and taking holidays, largely because of the spread of the railways, there was more demand for souvenirs of places visited. What better than a series of photographic views? Cheltenham, being a popular resort, had a number of photographers pass through, taking such pictures. The firms of Francis Frith, George Washington Wilson and John Valentine all produced photographs of the town, particularly during the 1880s.

The town-based photographers continued to concentrate mainly on portraiture. Although some outdoor photographs were taken of special events, the cumbersome equipment and complicated processing procedures made such work awkward. Between 1860 and 1890 there were over 50 different photographers who set up business in Cheltenham. Some only lasted a year or two, others a decade or more. This was the heyday of commercial photography and a fashionable, prosperous town provided a ready market of people eager to have their pictures taken.

In 1888 the first Kodak camera was produced. By the end of the century, the company had introduced roll film and hand-held cameras. Buying and using a camera was cheaper and easier than ever before. More people started taking their own 'snapshots' and amateur photography became a popular pastime. As a result, commercial photographers began to lose business and studios closed down.

The pictures that follow are a selection from the collection of Cheltenham Art Gallery and Museum. They are the work of both professional and amateur photographers who, through their lenses, captured Cheltenham in camera. Together they provide us with fascinating glimpses of the town and its people in the past.

FRONT COVER: Boys of the Cheltenham College Engineer Cadet Corps Band are pictured preparing for the parade that celebrated the College's fiftieth anniversary. In the distance are the mid-19th century College buildings.

LEFT: Louisa Strachan, photographed in the mid-1870s: the photographer was Richard Dighton, who had his studio at Weston Villa, 433 High Street, working as a photographer from 1865 until 1884. Louisa was one of the many Cheltenham residents who had 'carte-de-visite' photographs of themselves produced. RIGHT: Their popularity provided a useful way for the photographers to advertise their services.

Crowds in Lansdown Road after the passing of the Prince of Wales' procession, on 13 May 1897. He arrived at Lansdown Station and then travelled in a horse-drawn carriage to the Pittville Pump Room. Thence he proceeded on horseback to Prestbury Park, to review a parade of the Royal Gloucestershire Hussars. Throughout, the Prince was greeted enthusiastically, with crowds gathering to cheer as he passed by.

Christ Church in Malvern Road was built between 1837 and 1840. The stone used came from the Dodwell Hill Quarry at Whittington. The church was designed to serve the new residential estates of Lansdown and Bayshill, as well as the established hamlet of Alstone. The final cost was just over £18,000. The photograph is thought to have been taken during the 1870s.

Charles Phillips, the carriage builder, began his business in Suffolk Street during the early 1890s and retired there in the 1920s. The photograph shows the Phillips' house and attached workshops in about 1910.

St Luke's Church bazaar was held on 5 July 1906, in the grounds of Thirlestaine Hall. St Luke's was built between 1853 and 1854 in College Road, as a place of worship for pupils at the Gentlemen's College and residents of the Sandford area. Thirlestaine Hall was built between 1855 and 1857. Owned by a James Fox in 1906, it remained a family home until the 1930s. It was then converted into a hotel and in 1952 into offices.

The Gordon Lamp was erected by a group of Montpellier residents and named after General Gordon, killed at Khartoum in 1885. It was first lit by gas in May 1887 and is seen here before its conversion to electricity in 1899, which changed its appearance. In the background is the chemist's shop of Waite, Kite and Codling and at number 4 Montpellier Street, Mr Steel, the greengrocer.

In 1809 Henry Thompson opened the first Montpellier Pump Room; a wooden building from which visitors could obtain the spa waters. This was replaced in 1817 by the colonnaded Long Room seen in this view. Between 1825 and 1826 the Rotunda was added: a domed circular room designed by John Papworth. As the popularity of the spa waters declined in the later 19th century, the Rotunda became a venue for dances, concerts and other entertainments. This photograph was taken in 1901 by H. F. Giles, an enthusiastic amateur photographer.

Montpellier Walk is pictured in the early 1890s. From 1831 this part of the town began to develop as a popular shopping area. The shops here were built in the 1840s and replaced the tree-lined avenue that led up to Montpellier Spa. The spire in the background is that of St Andrew's Presbyterian Church, built in 1885.

Montpellier Walk, some 60 years later, was taken in the 1930s and shows elements of Cheltenham, both past and future. From the past there is the architecture, the horse's drinking trough and the statue of King Edward VII, erected in 1914. The future, in the shape of the motor car, comes up the hill past Montpellier Gardens. Today this road is all too often clogged with traffic. Note also the bath chair on the pavement outside the chemist's shop.

Montpellier Gardens were originally part of the attractions of Montpellier Spa. In 1893 the Council bought them as a town amenity. Although admission was free on Sundays, a charge of 3d was payable during the rest of the week. The elaborate iron gates and railings ensured that people did not get in easily without paying. This main entrance was In Montpellier Walk and is seen in 1912.

The Gardens, pictured in 1905, were used for concerts, recitals and open-air theatre. Popular sports, including tennis, croquet and archery were also enjoyed — by those who could afford them. The Cheltenham Archers were founded in 1857, annual subscription one guinea. They held meetings on alternate Wednesdays in the Gardens, as indicated by the archery butt. In 1934 the Council abolished the entrance fee and, for safety's sake, the Archers moved to a practice site in the Old Bath Road.

This arch was erected in Montpellier Walk in May 1897 for the visit of the Prince of Wales. A number were put up around the town on the route of the Prince's procession. Householders, businessmen and shopkeepers also decorated their premises with flags and bunting.

The Royal Gloucestershire Hussars parade in Montpellier Spa Road. The Hussars Permanent Duty was first held in Cheltenham in 1852. Until 1893 they used the Plough Hotel as their Headquarters, that year moving to the Queen's Hotel. With parades through the streets and a review at Prestbury Park, the townsfolk had plenty of opportunities to admire men and horses. This photograph was taken in about 1900.

Cheltenham Ladies' College and Montpellier Street were photographed here in the 1880s. The Ladies' College moved to this site in 1873 after outgrowing the premises at Cambray House, where it had opened in 1854. The Art and Music Wing, seen here, was completed in 1882.

A lantern slide shows the construction of the Princess Hall at the Ladies' College in 1897. The building demolished to make way for the new hall was the Old Well Pump Room, built between 1849 and 1850. It was on the site of the original well, where the first mineral water spring had been discovered in 1716.

The Promenade was laid out between 1817 and 1818 as a tree-lined walk. It led from the High Street up to the Sherborne Pump Room, which stood on the site now occupied by the Queen's Hotel. The photographer set up his camera next to the Hotel to take this 1860s view.

These motor cars took part in the 1000 Mile Automobile Club Trial, arriving at the Winter Gardens in April 1900. The Winter Gardens stood where the Imperial Gardens are now. Built in 1878 for concerts and exhibitions, they became a venue for roller skating, a cinema and theatre. After falling into disrepair during the 1930s, the building was demolished in 1942.

The 1000 Mile Trial was the first long-distance motor race in this country. It lasted 18 days, starting and finishing in London. On 25 April 1900 the competitors drove from Bristol to Birmingham, stopping for a lunch break in Cheltenham. The eventual race winner was the Honourable Charles Rolls, driving a 12-horse power Panhard-Levassor. The cars are seen here in Imperial Square, shortly before leaving for Birmingham.

LEFT: Part of Imperial Square, photographed about 1870. RIGHT: An officer of the Royal Gloucestershire Hussars leads his troop in Imperial Square in the late 1890s. In the background is Cambray Spa, opened in 1834. In 1873, with the demand for spas declining, it became a Turkish Bath, although the waters could still be taken. The building was demolished in 1938.

Crowds gather for the switching-on of the Neptune Fountain, 30 October 1893. It was built by R. L. Boultons, the local architectural sculptors, carvers and modellers. The water is pumped up from the River Chelt, which flows through culverts below ground at this point.

The Neptune Fountain was in full flow in about 1895. The terrace of houses to the left was built by Samuel Hawarden between 1823 and 1825. From 1914 the Borough Council began to acquire the central houses. These are now the Municipal Offices; other firms have taken over the rest of the terrace.

The corner of St George's Road and the Promenade in about 1905: from 1897 the gas lamps that had lit Cheltenham for some 70 years were gradually replaced by electric lights. In the wider streets, such as the Promenade and Lansdown Place, the lights were above the middle of the road, suspended from two lampposts.

This circus arrived in the town sometime in the late 1890s. The procession makes its way along the Promenade towards the High Street. In the background are the shops of Dale Forty and Company, piano sellers, and Henry Neale and Sons, a china and glass warehouse.

A view of St George's Road about 1890; on the left are the buildings of the Ladies' College. On the right is Royal Well Chapel.

The Promenade in about 1895, looking towards the junction with St George's Road and Imperial Square; one of the gas lamps can be clearly seen. Gas lighting was first introduced in the High Street in 1818. By 1845, Cheltenham was said to be 'one of the best lit towns in the Kingdom'.

In this view of the Lower Promenade, the old frontage of Cavendish House can be seen. It was in July 1826 that Thomas Clark and William Debenham opened their 'Silk Mercery Establishment' at 3 Promenade. This shop was a branch of a business which had begun with a London store. The Cavendish House Company was formed in 1888. The photograph dates to the 1920s.

In October 1928 the 63rd Annual Church Congress was held in Cheltenham. Some of the delegates leave the Promenade in procession. They were probably going to either St Matthew's Church in Clarence Street or St Mary's Church.

LEFT: Clarence Street in the 1860s — a view from the corner of Clarence Parade; in the distance is the temporary church, erected in 1859 when St Mary's had to be closed for structural repairs. Although the Parish Church reopened in 1861, the corrugated iron church continued to be used until 1877. RIGHT: St Matthew's Church was built between 1877 and 1884 on the site of the temporary church. Because it was too expensive to alter St Mary's it was decided to build a new church to accommodate more people. In 1952 the spire was removed after being declared unsafe. The tower was lowered for the same reason in 1972.

A view of Clarence Street taken in the early 1890s shows St Matthew's Church on the right, designed by Ewan Christian and built at a cost of £20,000. The people watching the photographer at work show that, even after 40 years, a man and a camera were something of a novelty on the streets of Cheltenham.

In April 1889 the building which housed the Free Library and the Schools of Art and Science was opened. This photograph, probably taken shortly after the opening, shows the gap (next to the Library's tower) where the Art Gallery was built in 1899. In 1907, the Schools of Art and Science were moved to St Margaret's Road. The rooms remaining above the Library were then taken over for use by the town's Museum.

A 1920s aerial photograph of the town: dominating the skyline are the spires of St Gregory's, St Matthew's and St Mary's. In the centre foreground are the buildings of what is now Shaftsbury Hall. Built in 1869 as St Mary's Hall, this was the female department of the Anglican Teacher Training College. The men used St Paul's College in Swindon Road.

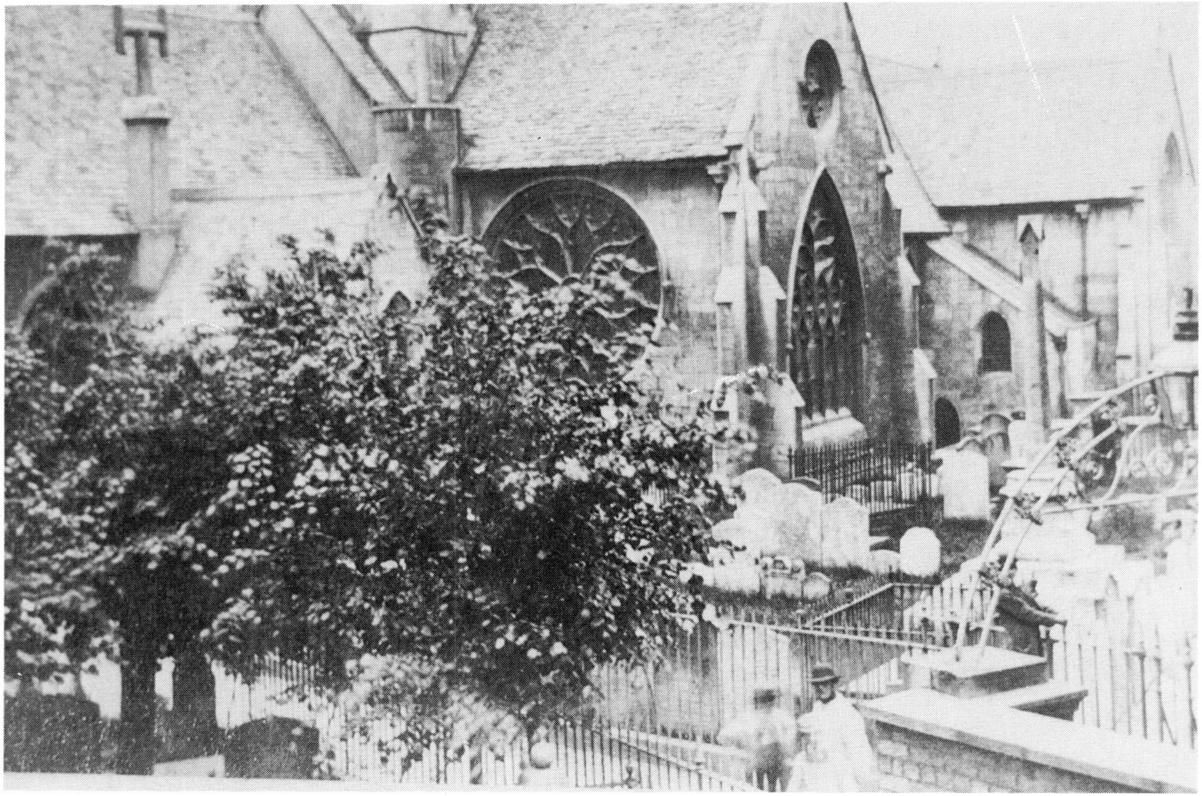

St Mary's Parish Church was photographed here about 1875. Most of the surviving fabric of the building is 14th century. There are however, two external buttresses at the west end and the pillars supporting the arches beneath the tower which are 12th century. The railings that are such a feature of the churchyard in this picture were removed during the Second World War.

LEFT: Ambrose Street and St Gregory's Roman Catholic Church are pictured here about 1920. Tram rails run up the middle of the road. The first electric trams, run by the Cheltenham and District Light Railway Company, began operating in August 1901. It was not until 1930 that they were replaced by the motor 'bus. RIGHT: The tower of St Gregory's Church was illuminated at night. Although building began in 1854, the church was not completed until 1876. It replaced a small Catholic chapel, built on the site between 1809 and 1810.

A 1920s view of the old police station in Crescent Place; originally this was the Clarence Hotel, named after the Duchess of Clarence, who later became Queen Adelaide. She had stayed there in August 1827. During the same visit Clarence Street received its name, as the Duchess travelled along the newly opened road to her accommodation. Until 1838, when the Queen's Hotel was opened, the Clarence was regarded as the town's finest place to stay. In 1858 it became the police station and it is now the headquarters of the Countryside Commission.

A crowd gathered at the junction of Clarence Street and the High Street to watch a procession. The shops behind the spectators are W. H. Davison, a jeweller's founded in 1828, and Bryant and Company, a tailor's. The photograph dates from about 1894.

This view of the High Street was taken from the junction with Clarence Street in the early 1890s. The closed shops suggest the picture was taken on a Sunday morning (the clocks read 11.35). In the centre, a group of children look into the window of G. R. Turner's shop. As Mr Turner was a confectioner, their interest is understandable. Other businesses on that side of the High Street included the glove manufacturing company of F. Heafield and the boot manufacturers, Stead and Simpson.

A sunny day in the High Street in about 1895; this is the corner of St George's Street. The shop opposite is that of the draper's, J. Dicks and Sons. The awnings are out to protect the stock from fading in the strong sunlight. The men in the foreground appear to be posing casually for the camera!

This photograph of the High Street shows (right) the junction with St George's Place, and (left) the castle-like frontage of the Grammar School. The first school on this site was the 16th century foundation of Richard Pate. The building was replaced in 1887 by the grand structure seen here. In 1965 the school moved to new premises in Princess Elizabeth Way. In 1967 the High Street thus witnessed its second demolition of a Grammar School, as this site was cleared to make way for shops.

The corner of Henrietta Street and the High Street in about 1893; the Fleece Hotel was a coaching house with a reputation for comfort and good living. For many years it was used as a meeting place by the Town Commissioners. Originally formed in 1786 'for paving the footways and passages in the town . . . and for better cleansing and lighting', the Commission served as the town's local government until 1876. In that year it was replaced by the Borough Council. The Fleece was demolished in 1967.

This aerial photograph shows the Henrietta Street brewery site about 1950. Brewing began here in 1760 when the original brewery was established by Thomas Gardner. In 1888 it became the Cheltenham Original Brewery Limited and in 1959 this company merged with the Stroud Brewery. The main buildings on the site date from 1898, the earlier brewery having been destroyed in a fire.

On 29 July 1816 the Duke of Wellington, victor at Waterloo, opened the new Assembly Rooms in the High Street. A ballroom, card and billiards rooms and a refreshment room were all available for the well-to-do. This view from about 1895 shows (left) the Assembly Rooms, with a 'Royal Salvo' tricycle outside. Next door, at number 390, is the tobacconist's shop of Titus Clee.

Another early 1890s view of the High Street; on the right is the Bell Hotel and next door, the shop of Mr J. R. Higgins, a trunk manufacturer. An advertisement in an early town guide celebrates the 'air tight tin cases for India and the Colonies' made by Higgins. Just beyond his shop is a gap in the line of buildings which is Winchcomb Street. The Penfold pillar box on the pavement dates from about 1866.

This view of the High Street dates to the 1920s and was taken from the same position as the picture on page 47. On the left is the Lloyds Bank building that was built in 1900 on the site of the Assembly Rooms. The Dragon and Onion electric lights, put up in place of the gas lamps in 1897, can be seen in the distance. Note also the overhead cable supports that line the High Street. These would be seen along the routes used by the electric trams.

The Plough Hotel was one of the oldest coaching inns in the High Street. In the early 19th century it took 10½ hours for a fast coach to get to London from the Plough. One left every morning. The large yard at the rear was used for stabling horses and the storage of coaches. It is seen here in about 1900 with men of the Royal Horse Artillery about to leave for a recruiting drive in the town. The site of the yard is now occupied by the Regent Arcade.

The corner of Cambray and the High Street photographed in 1893; the building on the left is the National Provincial Bank. On the right is the Royal Hotel, described in 1845 as one to 'make the English hotel the admiration of the world'. It is now the site of the Beechwood Place shopping arcade. Beyond are the premises of G. H. New, a tea and coffee merchant, and W. R. Wheatley, a sheet music seller.

The Gordon Boy's Brigade was formed in 1891. They are seen here on parade in the grounds of their headquarters. This was in Liverpool Place, just off the High Street and next to the Royal Hotel. This photograph was taken in the late 1890s.

Winchcomb Street, looking north, was photographed here in about 1897. In the distance are the twin towers of the Highbury Congregational Chapel, which had been built in the early 1850s and was closed in 1932. The Odeon Cinema now stands there. At the time the picture was taken the row of shops included: Mr R. Partridge, an umbrella maker, Mr Stone, a tea and coffee dealer, Miss Flory, a milliner and Mr Shrives, a watch and clockmaker.

Another view of Winchcomb Street in the late 1890s; the children are standing outside the milliner's shop of Miss Flory. Across the road are the premises of George Turk, a saddler, J. Huber, a jeweller, watch and clockmaker and G. H. Cane, a newsagent.

A workcart stands by one of the Winchcomb Street gas lamps, probably during repairs to the gas supply pipe. Across the road is the Central Domestic Agency, and next door the hay and straw dealers, Ride and Company. Further on along the street is Mr Deane, a tinsmith, and then the ironmongery and tool warehouse of John Fisher. In the distance can be seen the coach building firm of Mills and Son. The elderly gentleman is riding a 'Coventry Rotary Tricycle'. The picture was taken in about 1890.

LEFT: The first horse-drawn omnibus service began in June 1890. 'Buses ran between Lansdown Station and Pittville Gates. A 'bus at the north end of Winchcomb Street, (the Gates just out of the picture) has stopped outside the premises of A. C. and S. Billings. This firm of contractors was responsible for building the Free Library and Schools of Art and Science in Clarence Street. The photograph dates from about 1895. RIGHT: Pittville Gates are pictured in the early 1900s.

In 1830 Cheltenham's last spa opened — the Pittville Pump Room. Unfortunately, the interest in spas was declining and by 1888 the Pump Room was financially unviable. In 1890 the Borough Council bought the building and the gardens. They also purchased three and a half acres of the Marle Hill Estate, just across the Evesham Road. Work then began to convert this into a park. One of the major tasks was the extension and deepening of Capper's Pond, to turn it into a boating lake. This photograph shows the work in progress in about 1893.

Once the boating lake was finished it became a popular attraction in Pittville. Rowing boats and canoes could be hired and during the summer months a steam launch took people on trips around the lake. Here are the landing stage, and the launch, getting up steam in readiness for the next sailing. The photograph was taken about the turn of the century.

This view shows the ornamental lake in Pittville Gardens. During cold winters it was regularly used for ice skating. For the rest of the year feeding the swans was the main attraction. The picture dates from about 1900.

Prestbury Park, to the north of the town, was first used for horse-racing in 1831. It was also used by the Royal Gloucestershire Hussars as a parade ground, during their annual visits to Cheltenham. This view of a crowd gathered at the Park is thought to date to May 1897, when the Prince of Wales reviewed the Hussars. The Prince was to arrive at noon, but crowds started to form early in the morning. Refreshment stalls, such as the one seen here, no doubt did brisk business selling ice-cream, fruit and drinks.

In 1919, faced with a shortage of residential accommodation, the Council purchased over 100 acres of land in the Parish of St Mark. It built 600 new houses with roads named after poets. Further building subsequently took place and this photograph shows the estate in about 1960. In the top right of the picture are the buildings originally used during the Second World War by the United States Army Forces of Supply, that became part of GCHQ. St Mark's Church, built in the 1860s, is in the bottom left corner.

This view of Cheltenham from Leckhampton Hill was taken in the 1880s. To the right is the famous Devil's Chimney, popularly thought to rise straight from Hell. In reality, the Chimney was probably formed during the construction of one of the Leckhampton Quarry inclines in the late 18th century. These were designed to help get the blocks of stone down from the Quarry. The Hill itself was settled in the Iron Age and the remains of a hillfort can be seen there. This picture was taken by a photographer working for the George Washington Wilson Photographic Company.

Leckhampton as photographed in 1863; in the distance is the Church of St Peter and, nearer the photographer, are some of the outbuildings of Leckhampton Court. In the Domesday Book two manors are recorded. The 14th century Court is the successor to one of them. During the First World War, it was turned into a hospital for wounded soldiers. In the Second it became a prisoner-of-war camp. It has been a private school and is now owned by the Sue Ryder Foundation.

St Peter's Church in Leckhampton was founded in the 12th century. The nave, tower and sanctuary were built in the 14th century, probably under the direction of Sir John Gifford, who died in about 1330. Alterations were made in the 1830s to increase the accommodation but, by the mid-1860s, it was again too small. Consequently, restoration and enlargement took place between 1865 and 1866 at a cost of just under £2,300. These photographs were taken in about 1890.

LEFT: Captain J. R. Philips and RIGHT: Mr Robert Barrett of the 13th Company, Cheltenham Rifle Volunteers, were photographed by John Joyner at his studio in the High Street, in October 1867. Joyner worked as a photographer from 1865 until 1908.

Albert Woodward was pictured in August 1891 with the prizes he had won in 'cycling races that year. Woodward was a sheet-music dealer and, through his business, got to know Adolphus Von Holst. One of Adolph's children was Gustav, who was born in Cheltenham in 1874 and is well known as the composer of 'The Planets'. The photograph was taken by Jesse Holloway, a 'Portrait, Animal and Landscape Photographer', in his studio at 32 Cambray Place.

On 6 December 1905, at the Athletic Ground, now the site of Tom Price Close, Cheltenham Rugby Football Club played the New Zealand All Blacks. 8,000 spectators saw the home team lose 18-0. The visitors were, however, full of admiration for the way that Cheltenham played. After the match, the New Zealanders were invited to high tea at the Town Hall. Each player received a guide book to the town as a souvenir. The photograph shows the two teams before the game.

The first County cricket match to be played on the Cheltenham College ground took place in August 1872. In 1878 the Cricket Festival began, with two matches. In 1906 the number was increased to three. W. G. Grace was, for nearly three decades, the Gloucestershire star player, enthralling spectators with his batting and bowling ability. This photograph shows some of the crowd at a match being played on the College ground in the 1890s.

Cheltenham College was established in 1841 to provide an Anglican education for gentlemen's sons. From Monday 22 June until Sunday 28 1891, the College celebrated its fiftieth anniversary. On the Thursday afternoon the Military Department's Engineer Corps paraded. They were joined by the Malvern Artillery Cadet Corps, the Clifton Engineer Cadet Corps and the Marlborough Rifle Cadet Corps. After the inspection and drill, there was a final march-past before the troops were dismissed for tea. This photograph was taken by Phillip Parsons, who had established his photographic business in 1889.

An interior view of the Junior House workroom at Cheltenham College; it was completed in 1909 as part of the new Junior School. This was built in the grounds of Lake House, bought by the College in 1904. The house itself was converted into accommodation for the Principal.

Boys in the open steeplechase race at the Glyngarth School sports day in 1891; the school, in Douro Road near Christ Church, catered for boys aged from 6 to 15.

A 1903 group photograph of the staff and boys at Glyngarth School; parents paid £80 a year to have their sons educated. The fee for a day boy was £13 a year. There were facilities for cricket, football and tennis. Military drill was also a regular part of the school routine.

This view of Duke Street shows one of the Gould children being carried to the waiting horse-drawn ambulance. Charles Gould was a chimney sweep — one of eleven in the town in 1894. He started his business in 1891, living at 60 Duke Street. A year later he moved to number 30 and by 1896 the Gould family had moved back up the road to 57.

At the time of the First World War Cheltenham had schools, the racecourse buildings and private house converted to accommodate injured and convalescing soldiers. This particular group were from the New Court Red Cross Voluntary Aid Hospital in Lansdown Place. The photograph was taken on 30 June 1916 in Montpellier Gardens. The men held a party to celebrate a victory in a local shooting competition.

The staff and patients at New Court were photographed outside the hospital at Easter 1917. New Court was a private house before opening as a hospital in October 1914. The first patients were Belgian troops, wounded in the defence of their country. Within months, however, the hospital was nursing British, Canadian and French soldiers. In the first two years, 952 men were cared for. While convalescing, the patients played cricket and billiards, held shooting competitions, put on revues and concerts and helped on local farms.

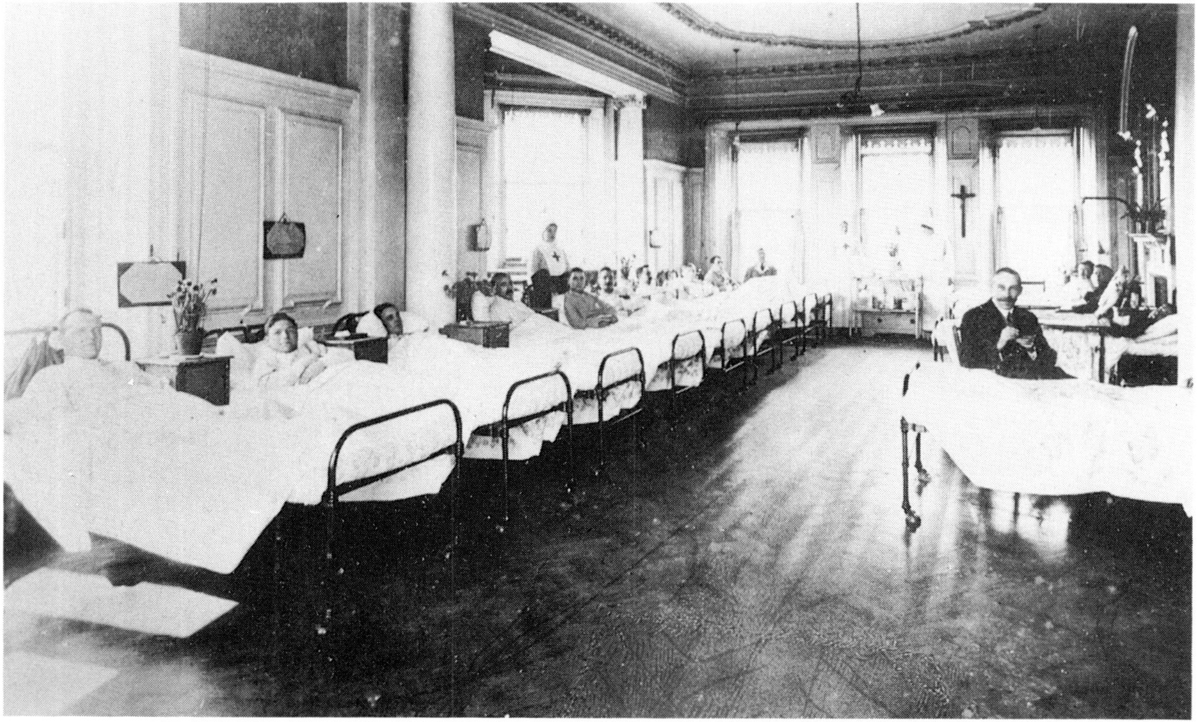

This is one of the wards at the New Court Hospital. There were 55 beds. In 1916, after the Battle of the Somme, the hospital was extended to help care for the increased numbers of wounded men. At first the dining-room was converted into a ward and meals were eaten in a tent in the garden. A wooden extension was then added to the building, paid for by Mr Herbert Unwin. This provided another 15 beds.

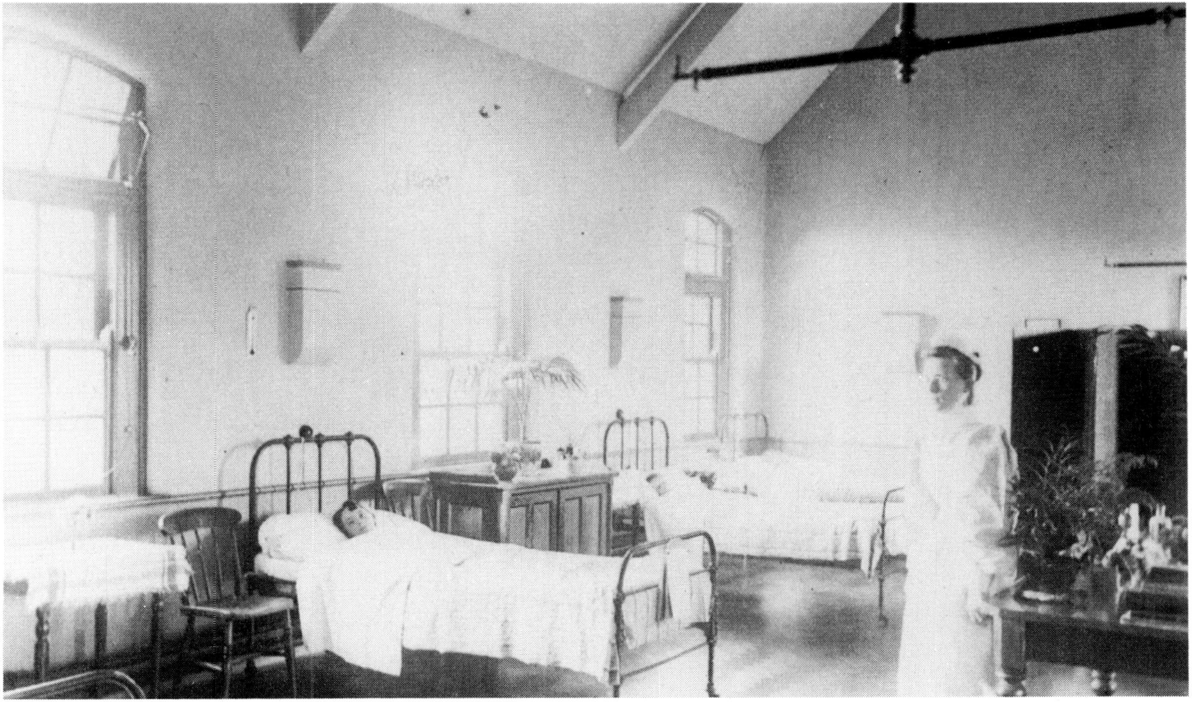

The Delancey Hospital for Infectious Disease was opened on 15 June 1874. The heirs of the late Miss Susan Delancey, who died in 1866, gave £5,000 towards the foundation of the hospital and private subscriptions boosted the funds available. The first wards to be completed were for those suffering from smallpox or scarlet fever. This photograph was taken by Dr J. H. Garrett, the town's Medical Officer of Health, about 1897.

Throughout the 1870s and 1880s successive Medical Officers urged the town's Public Health Committee to authorise the building of a public abbatoir. There were some 35 slaughterhouses in Cheltenham in 1890, almost every butcher having his own. The Medical Officers highlighted the problems of offensive smells, sewers clogged with animal remains and the difficulty of inspecting so many premises. This led to poor hygiene standards and infected meat was common. By 1892 it was agreed that an abbatoir should be built and it was opened the following year.

As part of the town's efforts to improve the public's health a steam disinfector was opened in 1892. It was next to the ash and refuse destructor on the Tewkesbury Road and was supplied by steam from a boiler heated by burning rubbish. The disinfector's main purpose was to stop the spread of infectious diseases. The bedding, mattresses and clothing of an infected person would be collected by the special vehicle. Once they had been treated they were returned; in serious cases they could be thrown straight into the fires of the destructor.

Index to Illustrations